The Prophets Graphically Presented

"Study to shew thyself approved unto God, a workman that needeth not to be ashamed, rightly dividing the word of truth."

2 Timothy 2:15

Copyright © 2018 Randy White
Cover and Illustration: Leonardo Costa

All rights reserved. This book or any portion thereof may not be reproduced or used in any manner whatsoever without the express written permission of the publisher except for the use of brief quotations in a book review.

Printed in the United States of America

First Edition, First Printing, 2018

ISBN: 978-1-945774-26-3

Dispensational Publishing House, Inc.
PO Box 3181
Taos, NM 87571

www.DispensationalPublishing.com

Ordering Information:
Quantity or wholesale discounts are available for churches, associations, and retailers. For details, contact the publisher.

1 2 3 4 5 6 7 8 9 10

CONTENTS

AN OVERVIEW OF THE TIMES AND THE PROPHETS

THE HEBREW SCRIPTURES - PART 1 4

THE HEBREW SCRIPTURES - PART 2 6

THE HEBREW SCRIPTURES - PART 3 8

THE NEVI'IM 10

WHERE AND WHEN 12

THE FORMULA OF PROPHETIC UTTERANCE 14

THE SEDARIM OF THE FORMER PROPHETS 16

THE PROPHETS TO THE OTHER NATIONS

THE PROPHET JONAH 20

WAS JONAH A REAL PERSON? 22

THE HIDDEN PROPHECY OF JONAH 24

THE PROPHET OBADIAH 26

THE PROPHET NAHUM 28

THE PROPHETS TO THE NORTHERN KINGDOM

THE PROPHET HOSEA 32

HOSEA'S SYMBOLIC CHILDREN 34

ARE THE GENTILES THE NEW AMMI? 36

THE PROPHET AMOS 38

A HARMONY OF PROPHECY

THE DAY OF THE LORD 42

THE GREAT TRIBULATION 44

THE JUDGMENT OF THE NATIONS 46

THE LEADERS OF WICKEDNESS 48

GOD'S VISIBLE MANIFESTATION OVER THE EARTH 50

BOOK BY BOOK

THE PROPHETIC CALL - PART 1 54

THE PROPHETIC CALL - PART 2 55

ISAIAH 56

JEREMIAH 57

LAMENTATIONS 58

EZEKIEL	59
DANIEL	60
HOSEA	61
JOEL	62
AMOS	63
OBADIAH	64
JONAH	65
MICAH	66
NAHUM	67
HABAKKUK	68
ZEPHANIAH	69
HAGGAI	70
ZECHARIAH	71
MALACHI	72

From the Author

Prophecy, like the night sky, has an intrigue that captures the mind and the imagination of young and old. And, like the night sky, it is an area of study that is filled with myth and legend as well as facts and reality. As students of the Word, our job is to separate the myth, shrouded in mystery, from the facts that are displayed in the Word and unfolding in history.

I hope you'll take these charts and use them as you go on a prophetic journey through time, using the ancient Hebrew prophets and the oracles they received from God as your guide.

You will see prophecy that has already been fulfilled. You will see prophecy that is yet future. Some prophecy is now perfectly clear while other prophecy we struggle to understand. But the journey through prophecy fulfilled and future, clear and mysterious, will help us understand our God as One who has meticulous accuracy, perfect understanding, and the goal of restoring all things.

In the pages that follow you have charts that will, I pray, help you in the journey.

Randy White,
Taos, NM

AN OVERVIEW OF THE TIMES AND THE PROPHETS

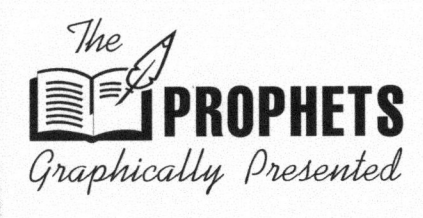

THE HEBREW SCRIPTURES - PART 1

The layout of our "Old Testament" is according to Roman Catholic tradition and not inspiration of God.

THE TORAH		
HEBREW NAME	HEBREW MEANING	ENGLISH NAME
Bereshith	"At the head" (Gen. 1:1)	Genesis
Shemot	"Names" (Ex. 1:1)	Exodus
Vayikra or "Torat Kohanim"	"He called" (Lv. 1:1) or "The Priestly Book"	Leviticus
Bamidbar	"In the wilderness" (Num. 1:1)	Numbers
Devarim	"words" (Deut. 1:1)	Deuteronomy

Notes

THE HEBREW SCRIPTURES - PART 2

The layout of our "Old Testament" is according to Roman Catholic tradition and not inspiration of God.

THE NEVI'IM		
HEBREW NAME	HEBREW MEANING	ENGLISH NAME
Yehoshua		Joshua
Shofetim		Judges
Shemuel		1 & 2 Samuel
Melakim		1 & 2 Kings
Yeshayahu		Isaiah
Yirmeyahu		Jeremiah
Yekhezqel		Ezekiel
Trei Asar	The Twelve	Hosea – Joel – Amos – Obediah – Jonah – Micah – Nahum – Habakkuk – Zephaniah – Haggai – Zechariah – Malachi

Notes

THE HEBREW SCRIPTURES - PART 3

The layout of our "Old Testament" is according to Roman Catholic tradition and not inspiration of God.

THE KETUVIM		
HEBREW NAME	HEBREW MEANING	ENGLISH NAME
Tehillim	Praises	Psalms
Mishlei	Proverbs	
Iyov	Job	
Shir Hashirim	Song of Songs	Song of Solomon
Rut	Ruth	
Eikhah	"How" (Lam. 1:1)	Lamentations
Qoheleth	"Preacher"	Ecclesiastes
Esther	Esther	
Daniel	Daniel	
Ezra-Nehemiah	Ezra / Nehemiah	
Divrei Hayamim	"The matters of the days"	1 & 2 Chronicles

Notes

THE NEVI'IM

THE FORMER PROPHETS - ZECHARIAH 7:7		THE LATTER PROPHETS	
BOOK	TOPIC	BOOK	TOPIC
Joshua	Settlement under the priesthood	Isaiah	God's entire view on Israel
Judges	Failure under the priesthood	Jeremiah	God's displeasure with Judah's sin
1 & 2 Samuel	Selltlement under kings	Ezekiel	God's judgment on Israel and the nations and ultimate blessing
1 & 2 Kings	Failure under kings	The Twelve	Judgment and future blessing

The latter prophets are divided into 21 sedarim for the public reading of Scripture. The 21 divisions are totally unrelated to the English arrangement of books.

Notes

WHERE AND WHEN

THE TIMELINE	THE NORTH	THE SOUTH	BEYOND	PERIOD	
850	-	Joel	-	Began ministry prior to the fall of Israel	
800	-	-	Jonah		
780-722	Hosea	-	-		■ Israel destroyed 722 BC
760	Amos	-	-		
745-690	Isaiah	Isaiah	-		
750-700	-	Micah	-	Began ministry prior to the fall of Judah	
701	-	Nahum	-		
639-609	-	Zephaniah	-		
612-605	-	Habakkuk	-		■ First exiles 605 BC
605-636	-	Daniel	-	Began ministry during the exile	
592-570	-	Ezekiel	-		
586-531	-	-	Obadiah		■ Jerusalem falls 586 BC
520	-	Haggai	-	Began ministry after the return of the exiles	
520	-	Zechariah	-		
432	-	Malachi	-		

Notes

THE FORMULA OF PROPHETIC UTTERANCE

Ignore chapters and verses and look for these markers

FORMULA	"The Word of the Lord"	Son of Man	Hear | Awake | Ho!	Woe | Burden	"The word of the Lord by" | "Hear the word of the Lord" | "The burden of the Lord"
FOUND	Jeremiah & Ezekiel	Ezekiel	Isaiah (when the prophecy is to the Jews)	Isaiah (when the prophecy is to the wicked or the surrounding nations)	The Minor (latter) prophets
EXAMPLES	Jeremiah 1:11, 13, 2:1 – total of 52 | Ezekiel 1:3, 6:3 – total of 60	Ezekiel 3:16-17 – total of 93	Isaiah 1:2, 10, 15 – total of 44	Isaiah 5:8, 11, 18, 20 – total of 21	Hosea 1:1, Joel 1:1 – total of 32

At times given in repetition within divisions

Notes

THE SEDARIM OF THE FORMER PROPHETS

The Hebrew text has our 12 "Minor Prophets" divided into 21 public readings, without regard to our books.						
Hos. 1:1-5:15	Hos. 6:1-10:11	Hos. 10:12-14:6	Hos. 14:7-Joel 2:26	Joel 2:27-Amos 2:9	Amos 2:10-5:13	Amos 5:14-7:14
Amos 7:15 - Obad. 20	Obad. 21-Jonah 4:11	Mic. 1:1-4:4	Mic. 4:5-7:19	Mic. 7:20-Nah. 3:19	Hab. 1:1-3:19	Zeph. 1:1-3:19
Zeph. 3:20-Hag. 2:22	Hag. 2:23-Zech. 4:1	Zech. 4:2-6:13	Zech. 6:14-8:22	Zech. 8:23-11:17	Zech. 12:1-14:20	Zech. 14:21-Mal. 4:6

Notes

THE PROPHETS TO THE OTHER NATIONS

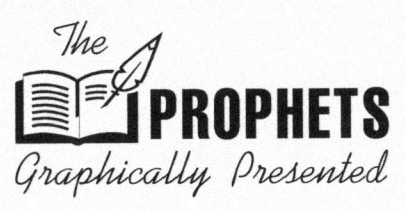

THE PROPHET JONAH

God's Word Comes to Jonah | 1:1	God's Word Comes to Jonah | 3:1
The Mission Announced | 1:2	The Mission Announced | 3:2
Jonah Disobeys | 1:3	Jonah Obeys | 3:3-4
Punishment and Resurrection | 1:4-2:10	Punishment and Correction | 3:4-4:11

Notes

WAS JONAH A REAL PERSON?

THE LIBERAL POSITION			THE BIBLICAL POSITION			
"To call this a 'historical account' turns attention away from the narrative itself"	The genre short story asks that each reader be open to enjoy, experience, and learn from the narrative. That learning is not prescribed ahead of time. Its discernment and application is entrusted to the community of faith. Indeed, candid and careful listening to Jonah's story may open our ears, perhaps enabling us to hear voices in our midst that have been quiet or overlooked.	A literal rendering of "one day" can be misleading because it might suggest a specific day and time when the Lord spoke.	The times, names, and places are presented as historical	2 Kings 14:23-27 is presented as historical	The New Testament mentions of Jonah are presented as historical, including connection with the Queen of Sheba (Matt. 12:38-42)	The Gospel of John mentions seven times that the words Jesus speaks are from God. (John 7:16, 8:28, 8:46-47, 12:49, 14:10, 14:24, 17:98)
Eugene F. Roop. *Ruth, Jonah, Esther, Believers Church Bible Commentary* (Scottdale, PA: Herald Press, 2002), p. 97.		Brynmor F. Price and Eugene Albert Nida. *A Translators' Handbook on the Book of Jonah*, UBS Handbook Series (Stuttgart: United Bible Societies, 1978), 48.				

Notes

THE HIDDEN PROPHECY OF JONAH

The book of Jonah only has one explicit prophecy: Jonah 3:4. The remaining prophecy is in type.

The typology of the resurrection of Christ	The typology of the resurrection of Israel							
Matthew 12:39-40 - which verifies the usage of types in the book of Jonah and also shows one of the types. (Compare also Luke 24:27).	Called	Disobedient	In trouble in the sea (compare Isaiah 57:20-21 & Deuteronomy 28:64-67 and the sea= gentiles-Rev 17:15)	Haven't forgotten identity - Jonah 1:9	Cast off (Rom. 11:12)	Casting away brought salvation to Gentiles (Compare Jonah 1:16 to Rom. 11:15)	Preserved and safe (and alive) within the sea	Sent again and used to restore the nations - Micah 4:2-8
	The book of Jonah is read on the Day of Atonement becauese the Jewish people recognize this typology							

The book of Jonah is not about the evangelism of the gentiles

Bibsac 108: Gerald B. Stanton, "The Prophet Jonah and His Message," Bibliotheca Sacra 108 (1951): 248.

Notes

THE PROPHET OBADIAH

THE FINAL VICTORY OVER ISRAEL'S MOST PERSISTENT ENEMY

Edom's Destruction	verses 1-16	"You Shouldn't have"	A reminder of Genesis 12:3	Israel's Restoration	Verses 17-21

Other Prophecies Against Edom

Isaiah 34:5-17	Jeremiah 49:17-22	Ezekiel 25:12-14, 35:1-15	Malachi 1:3-4

Has Edom Been Destroyed?

Obadiah 1:10 promises it	There are *no* people nor land called Edom today. BUT, the *idumeans* were the Edomites forced into Jewish conversion during the Maccabean era.	Isaiah 34:5-17

Notes

THE PROPHET NAHUM

FOLLOWING UP ON NINEVAH

| Ninevah was the capital of Assyria, which had conquered the Kingdom of Israel in 722BC | Jonah had prophesied in Ninevah approx. 87 years earlier. The repentance at that time had delayed judgment. | Nahum prophesied with vivid description of the coming destruction of Nineveh. | 115 Years after Nahum, the city was utterly destroyed, fulfilling the prophetic word. |

Notes

THE PROPHETS TO THE NORTHERN KINGDOM

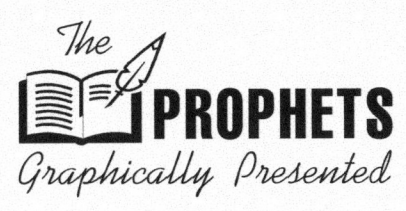

THE PROPHET HOSEA

INTRODUCTION | 1:1	SYMBOLIC | 1:2-3:5		LITERAL | 4:1-14:8		CONCLUSION | 14:9
"The word of the LORD that came unto Hosea"	The First Wife | 1:2-2:23	The Second Wife | 3:1-3:5	Incriminations | 4:1-5:15 ⇓ Resolve to Return | 6:1-3	Incriminations | 6:4-18:8 ⇓ Invitation to Return | 13:9-14:8	"…the ways of the LORD *are* right…"

The book of Hosea covers a period of time greater than 70 years, from Jeroboam's Reign to the fall of Samaria.

Notes

HOSEA'S SYMBOLIC CHILDREN

JEZREEL | 1:4-5		LO-RUHAMAH | 1:6-9		LO-AMMI | 1:8-9	
Meaning	Significance	Meaning	Significance	Meaning	Significance
May God Scatter - May God Sow	Israel will be scattered in Jezreel.	Not Beloved - See Rom. 9:25 & 1 Peter 2:10	God will show no compassion on Israel, but will on Judah	Not My People	God is going to reject Israel and separate Himself from them.

Notes

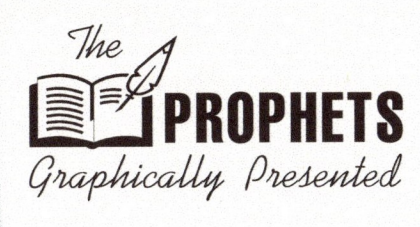

ARE THE GENTILES THE NEW AMMI?

A common interpretation of Romans 9:24-25 is that the Jews are now *Lo Ammi* and the church is *Ammi*.

"Even us, whom he hath called, not of the Jews only, but also of the Gentiles?" (Rom. 9:24).	"…I will call them my people, which were not my people…" (Rom 9:25).
"…us, whom he hath called" is the key. The entire chapter has been exclusively about the elect nation, without one word about elect individuals.	Both the words Jew and Gentile are anachronisms, coming to their current meaning only centuries after Paul. The text says "Judean" and "of the nations" (i.e.: scattered).	The context of a quoted verse of Scripture cannot be ignored in the place it is quoted. Since the context of Paul's quote relates solely to Israel, the application cannot mean "the church." To make such out-of-context application would be gross misuse of Paul's writing of Scripture.

Notes

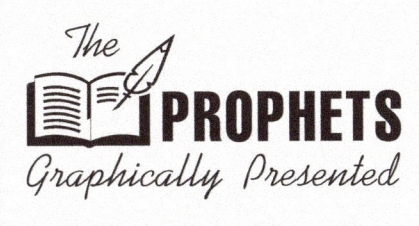

THE PROPHET AMOS

LITERAL PROPHECY | 1:1-6:14		SYMBOLIC PROPHECY | 7:1-9		LITERAL PROPHECY | 7:10-17	
To Israel, Judah, and others | 1:1-2:16	To Israel alone | 3:1-6:14	Grasshoppers | 7:1-3	Judgment averted: It "shall not be" (7:3, 6)	Amos threatened with captivity | 7:10-13	Amos' defense and counter threat of captivity | 7:14-17
		Fire | 7:4-6			
		Plumbline | 7:7-9			
		All judgment averted | 7:3, 6, 8			

SYMBOLIC PROPHECY | 8:1-3		LITERAL PROPHECY | 8:4-14		SYMBOLIC PROPHECY | 9:1-4		LITERAL PROPHECY | 9:5-15	
The Symbol	The Significance	The heinous state of affairs | 8:4-6	The prophesied result | 8:7-13	Smite the lintel! | 9:1	There is no escape! | 9:1-4	Exile from the land | 9:5-10	Restoration to the land | 9:11-15
A basket of summer fruit | 8:1-2	The rot will soon set in | 8:2-3	Charge to those who believe it is the right path | 8:14					

Notes

A HARMONY OF PROPHECY

With gratitude for the work of Arno C. Gaebelein. These charts were compiled with information contained in "*The Harmony of the Prophetic Word: A Key to Old Testament Prophecy Concerning Things to Come*" (New York: "Our Hope" Publication Office, 1907).

THE DAY OF THE LORD

SEEN IN SHADOWS	SEEN EXPLICITLY				
	Former Prophets			Latter Prophets	
Numbers 24:17	Isaiah	Jeremiah	Ezekiel	Obadiah 15	Micah 5:5
Deuteronomy 32:41-43	2:12-21, 4:1-6, 10:5-34, 11:1-16, 13:9-13, Chapters 24-27	25:30-33, 30:18-24	13:5	Joel 1:5, 2:1-2, 2:10-11, 2:30-31, 3:14-16	Zephaniah 1:1-14, 2:1–3, 8–15; 3:11, 16
1 Samuel 2:10				Hosea 11:9-11	Malachi 4:1-3

Notes

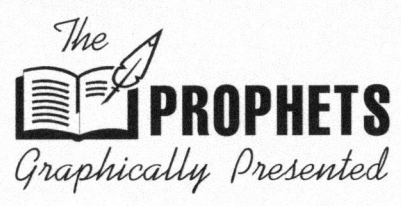

THE GREAT TRIBULATION

SEEN IN TYPE	SEEN IN INDIRECT PROPHECY			SEEN IN DIRECT PROPHECY
Genesis 15:12	Deuteronomy 32:15, 35, 36	The "Remnant" Psalms, including 43:1-2, 59:1-3 The "Remnant" Psalms, including 43:1-2, 59:1-3	Joel 2:17-19	Jeremiah 30:4-8
Joseph sold to Egypt			Hosea 5:14, 6:1-3	Daniel 12:1
The Egypt experience			Isiah 59:19-20	Zechariah 14:1-3
			Ezekiel 21:27	Matthew 24:21-22
			Micah 7:1-7	
			Habakkuk 3:16	

44

Notes

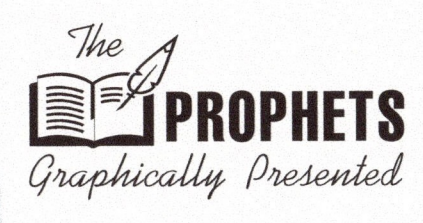

THE JUDGMENT OF THE NATIONS

The Peculiar Nation	Times of the Gentiles	The Invincibility of the Jewish Nation	The Nations Judged for their treatment of Israel	The final battle over Jerusalem
Amos 3:2	Jeremiah 27:6-7	Numbers 23:23-24	Joel 3:2-4, 12	Daniel 12:2,3,9
Exodus 19:5-6	Zechariah 1:19 (in conjunction with Daniel 2)	Psalm 2:1-3	Isaiah 29:1-8	Zechariah 14:2-5, 12-15
Deuteronomy 10:15		Psalm 46:6-7	Isaiah 34:1-3	
Jeremiah 31:35		Psalm 83:1-6	Isaiah 66:24	
Romans 11:29			Jeremiah 25:13-17	
			Revelation 19:17-18	

Notes

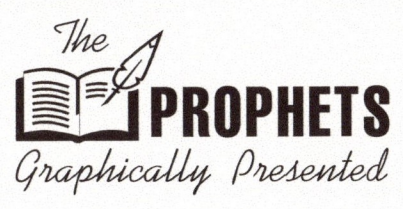

THE LEADERS OF WICKEDNESS

THE ROMAN EMPIRE	THE ANTICHRIST
"…if another shall come in his own name, him ye will receive" John 5:43	
Daniel 2	Genesis 3:15
	Numbers 24:7
	Deuteronomy 32:42
	Psalm 10:1-11, 37:10-11, 43:1
	Isaiah 30:31-33
	Ezekiel 28:1-19
Revelation 14	Daniel 7, 11:36-38
	Micah 5:4-5
	Nahum 1:11-14
	Zehariah 11:15-17
	Joel 2:20
	2 Thessalonians 2:3-13

Notes

GOD'S VISIBLE MANIFESTATION OVER THE EARTH

IN THE TORAH	IN THE PSALMS	IN THE PROPHETS	IN THE NEW TESTAMENT
Exodus 13:21, 14:24, 16:10	Psalm 18*	Joel 3:11	Matthew 16:27-28, 17:1-2
Exodus 19:16-18	Psalm 29:3-9	Isaiah 2:19	Matthew 24:30
Numbers 11:25, 12:5	Psalm 50	Isaiah 4	Acts 1:11
Deuteronomy 33:1-2	Psalm 68	Isaiah 10:33-34, 11:4, 25:9, 30:27-30	Revelation 19:11-16
	Psalm 76	Isaiah 33:17, 40:5, 63:1-4	In conclusion we wish to remark that the coming of the Lord, the blessed Hope of the church, is something entirely different from the visible and glorious manifestation of the Lord. The blessed Hope is our gathering together unto Him. (2 Thess. 2:1.) Such a Hope is not revealed in the Old Testament, for the church was then unrevealed. Arno C. Gaebelein, The Harmony of the Prophetic Word: A Key to Old Testament Prophecy Concerning Things to Come (New York: "Our Hope" Publication Office, 1907), 103.
	*It is a superficial Bible study which can claim a fulfilment of this Psalm in the experience of King David Arno C. Gaebelein, The Harmony of the Prophetic Word: A Key to Old Testament Prophecy Concerning Things to Come (New York: "Our Hope" Publication Office, 1907), 103.	Ezekiel 1:26-28, 43:1-4	
		Daniel 7:13	
		Habakkuk 2:15, 3:1-18	
		Zechariah 9:9-10, 12:10, 14:5	
		Malachi 4:2-3	

Notes

BOOK BY BOOK

The book overview charts on pages 58 to 76 are courtesy of Dr. Kenneth G. Hanna, from his excellent survey of the Old Testament, "*From Moses to Malachi*."
Copyright 2015, Kenneth G. Hanna. Used by permission.

THE PROPHETIC CALL - PART 1

1. Began with a personal encounter with God.
- Isaiah 6:1–8
- Jeremiah 1:4–10
- Ezekiel 1–3
- Amos 7:14–15

2. Sometimes came early, sometimes late in life.
- Early: Isaiah, Jeremiah
- Amos, Haggai

3. Sometimes involved a long career, sometimes a short career.
- **Long:**
  Isaiah – at least 58 years (730–681 B.C.)
  Jeremiah – at least 45 years (627–582 B.C.)
- **Short:**
  Amos – approx. 1 year (762 B.C.)
  Haggai – 3 months (520 B.C.)

4. Often occurred in crisis times.
- **Isaiah:** death of Uzziah, invasion by Assyria
- **Jeremiah:** invasion by Babylon, fall of Jerusalem
- **Ezekiel:** deportation to Babylon
- **Joel:** locust plague
- **Haggai:** return of Jews from Babyblon

By Kenneth G. Hanna

THE PROPHETIC CALL - PART 2

5. Frequently opposed and persecuted.
- **Jeremiah:** plotted against, imprisoned, beaten (Jeremiah 18:18, 23; 20:2; 37:15)
- **Daniel:** captive, survived a death sentence (Daniel 6:16–18)

6. Often came at great personal cost.
- **Ezekiel:** captive in Babylon, his wife died (Ezek. 24:15-19)
- **Jeremiah:** despaired of life (Jeremiah 20:14-18)
- **Isaiah:** tradition says he was sawed in half (Hebrews 11:32)
- **Hosea:** his wife became a prostitute (Hosea 1:2)

7. Met with resistance:
- Isaiah – 1:5
- Jeremiah – 1:6–8
- Jonah – 1:3; 4:1–3

8. Aways accompanied by divine enablement/compulsion:
- Isaiah – 6:6–8
- Jeremiah – 1:9–10
- Ezekiel – 2:1–2; 3:8
- Amos – 3:8

By Kenneth G. Hanna

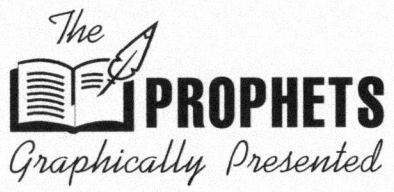

ISAIAH

Key Words:
Redemmer,
Holy One of Israel,
In that day,
My Servant,
Judgment,
Salvation,
Comfort,
Glory

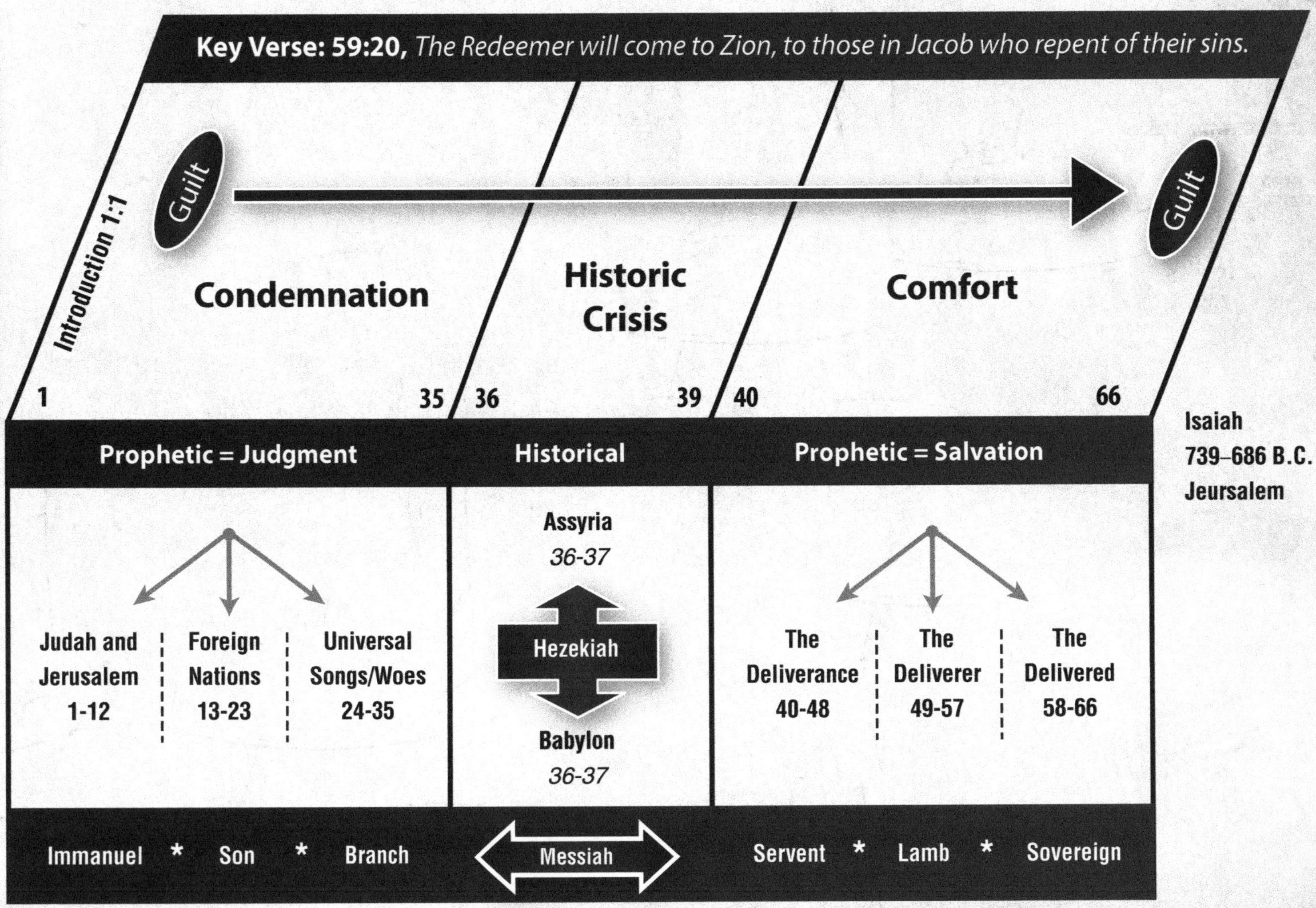

Key Verse: 59:20, *The Redeemer will come to Zion, to those in Jacob who repent of their sins.*

Introduction 1:1 | Guilt → Guilt

Condemnation	Historic Crisis	Comfort
1 — 35	36 — 39	40 — 66
Prophetic = Judgment	Historical	Prophetic = Salvation
Judah and Jerusalem 1-12 · Foreign Nations 13-23 · Universal Songs/Woes 24-35	Assyria 36-37 / Hezekiah / Babylon 36-37	The Deliverance 40-48 · The Deliverer 49-57 · The Delivered 58-66
Immanuel * Son * Branch	← Messiah →	Servent * Lamb * Sovereign

Isaiah
739–686 B.C.
Jeursalem

By Kenneth G. Hanna

JEREMIAH

Key Words:
Babylon,
Against,
Return,
Punish,
Restore

Key Verse: 25:11, *These nations will serve the king of Babylon seventy years.*

Judgment Prophesied

Jeremiah's Call	On Judah, Jerusalem	Jerusalem falls to Babylon	On the Nations	Jeremiah's Fall
1	2		45 / 46	51 52

↓ 39

Jeremiah with Baruch 627–586 B.C.

Timing	Judgment Announced Prophecies Given Before		Judgment Accomplished— Prophecies Given After	
Target nation	Prophecies Against Judah During the Reigns of:			Prophecies Against: Egypt, Philisita, Moab, Ammon, Edom, etc., 46–49, Babylon 50–51
	Josiah and Jehoahaz 2–20	Jehoiakim and Zedekiah 21–39	Gedaliah 40–45	
Key chapters	18 The Potter and the Clay	25, 29 The Seventy-Year Captivity	31 The New Covenant	36 The Indestructible Word of God

By Kenneth G. Hanna

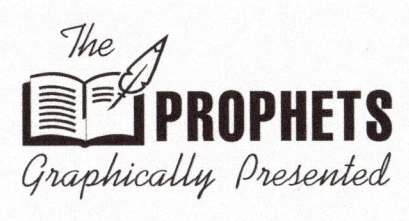

LAMENTATIONS

Key Words:
Affliction,
Compassion,
Anger,
Down,
Comfort,
Hope

Key Verses: 3:22-23, *Because of the Lord's great love we are not consumed, for his compassions never fail. They are new every morning; great is thy faithfulness.*

Zion's Affliction	Lord's Anger	Jeremiah's Response	People's Desperation	Plea for Mercy
1	2	3	4	5
Cause	**Consequence**	**Confidence**	**Condition**	**Call**
Jerusalem has sinned	The Lord has judged	He will show compassion	People waste away	Restore us O Lord!
Prayer 1:20-22	Prayer 2:20-22	Prayer 3:55-66	Promise 4:22	Prayer 5:1-22

The Lord's Unfailing Love

Jeremiah
586 B.C.
Jerusalem

By Kenneth G. Hanna

The Prophets Graphically Presented

EZEKIEL

Key Words:
Sovereign LORD,
They will know,
I am the LORD,
Son of man,
Temple,
Glory

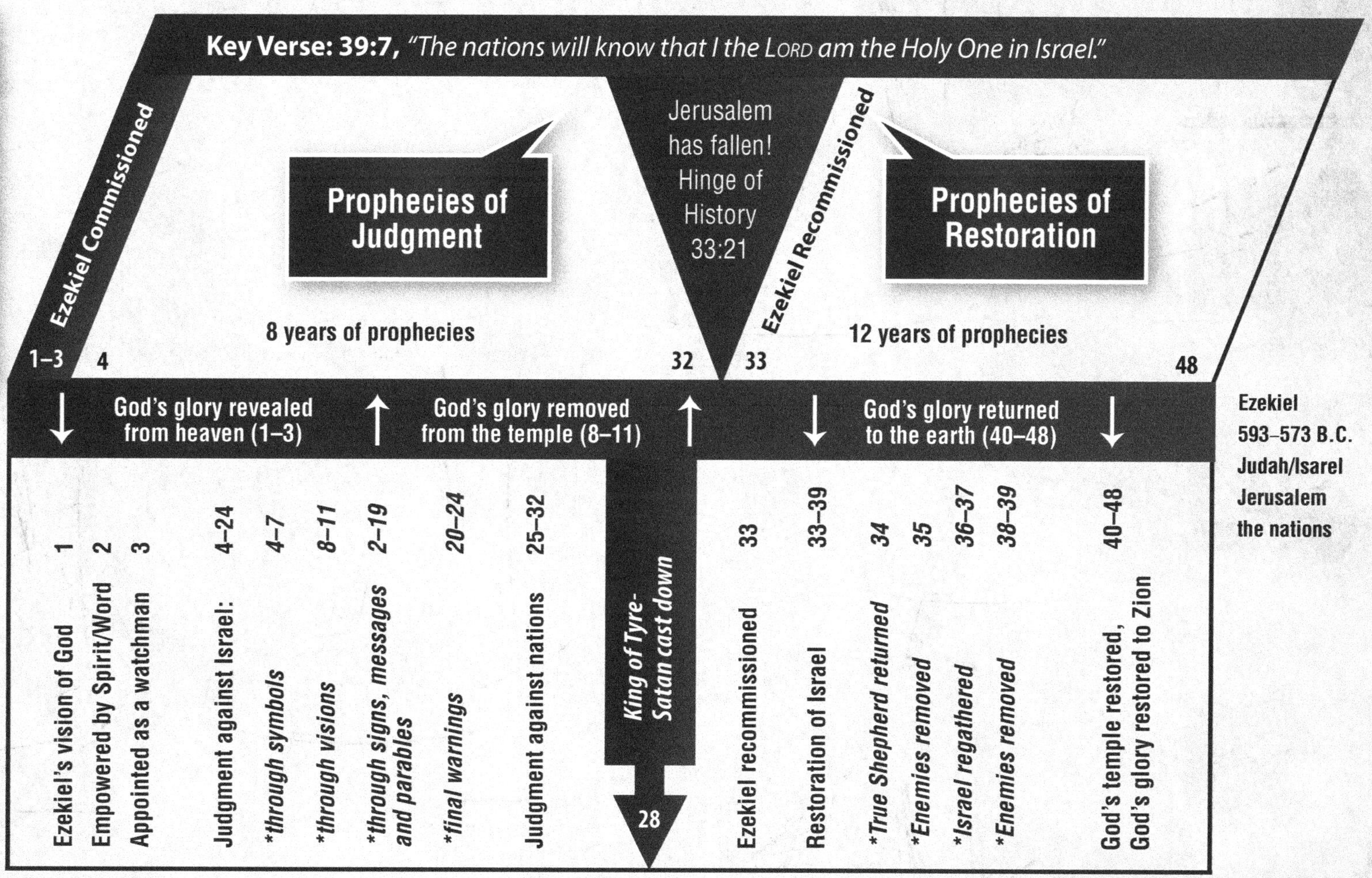

Key Verse: 39:7, "The nations will know that I the LORD am the Holy One in Israel."

Ezekiel Commissioned

Prophecies of Judgment

Jerusalem has fallen! Hinge of History 33:21

Ezekiel Recommissioned

Prophecies of Restoration

8 years of prophecies

1–3 | 4 | 32 | 33 | 48

12 years of prophecies

God's glory revealed from heaven (1–3) ↓ ↑ God's glory removed from the temple (8–11) ↑ ↓ God's glory returned to the earth (40–48) ↓

Ch	Content
1	Ezekiel's vision of God
2	Empowered by Spirit/Word
3	Appointed as a watchman
4–24	Judgment against Israel:
4–7	*through symbols
8–11	*through visions
2–19	*through signs, messages and parables
20–24	*final warnings
25–32	Judgment against nations
28	King of Tyre - Satan cast down
33	Ezekiel recommissioned
33–39	Restoration of Israel
34	*True Shepherd returned
35	*Enemies removed
36–37	*Israel regathered
38–39	*Enemies removed
40–48	God's temple restored, God's glory restored to Zion

Ezekiel
593–573 B.C.
Judah/Israel
Jerusalem
the nations

By Kenneth G. Hanna

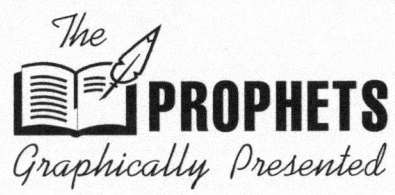

DANIEL

Key Words:
Kingdom(s),
Dominion,
Dream(s),
Vision(s),
Beasts

Key Verse: 4:17, *So that the living may know that the Most High is sovereign over the kingdoms of men.*

God is Sovereign!

	Prophetic History of the Gentile Nations	Prophetic History of Israel under Gentiles
Israel Captive in Babylon	2 — 7	8 — 12

Hebrew (1:2–3)	Aramaic (Chaps. 2:4–7:28)	Hebrew (Chaps. 8–12)

1	*Dreams and images of others*							*Daniel's Vision*		
Daniel captive in Babylon	2 Nebuchadnezzar's image: Four Gentile kingdoms	3 Nebuchadnezzar's image of gold = the fiery furnace	4 Nebuchadnezzar's tree: dream and humiliation	5 Belshazzar's feast and fall	6 Darius, Medes, and Persians Daniel in the lion's den	7 Vision of the four beasts		8 The Ram and the Goat Persia and Greece = near	9 The Seventy Weeks Times of the Gentiles = far	10–12 Panorama of the Future

Daniel
605–535 B.C.
Israel and
Gentile Nations

By Kenneth G. Hanna

HOSEA

Key Words:

Adulterers,
Covenant-broken,
Lovers,
Return,
Love

Key Verse: 3:1, *Love her as the L*ORD *loves the Israelites, though they turn to other gods.*

Hosea's Prodigal Wife
Gomer

God's Prodigal People
Israel (and Judah)

| 1 | | 3 | 4 | | | 14 |

1	2	3	4–5	6:1–3	6–13	14:1–9
Marriage to Gomer (Representing Israel)	**Rejection of Israel** (Gomer in background)	**Restoration of Gomer** (Predictive of Israel)	**Recounting Israel's Sin** (Spiritual apostasy = Adultery)	**"Repentance" of Israel** (Outward and inadequate)	**Response of the Lord** — *Plea for real repentence *Promised judgment 6 *Privileged past 7:1–9:9 *Persistent adultery 9:10–11:11 11:12–13:16	**Return and Restoration of Israel Promised**

Hosea
760–710 B.C.
Israel

By Kenneth G. Hanna

JOEL

Key Words:

Day of the Lord,
Return to me,
Locust, Army,
My Spirit,
Nations,
Holy

Key Verse: 2:1, *Sound the alarm on my holy hill - for the day of the LORD is coming. It is close at hand.*

Prophetic Revelation

- Mourning at Devastation
- Return to the LORD your God
- Rejoicing at Deliverance

Historic Invasion

Locusts → Northern army → the LORD will roar from Zion

1   2:1   3:21

Awful plague now → Worse coming in the future → Restoration is possible → Finally, the day of the LORD is coming

Joel
830 B.C.
Judah and
Jerusalem

| Devastation by locusts: 1:2–14 (Past) | Dreadful day of the LORD: 1:15 (Future) | Drought following locusts: 1:16–20 (Present) | Invasion by nothern army: 2:1–11 (Imminent) | Invitation from the LORD 1:12–17 (Timeless) | Intervention by the LORD Spirit will be poured out 2:18–32 (Future) | Indignation on all nations 3:1–16 (Distant) | Institution of millennium 3:17–21 (Ultimate) |

By Kenneth G. Hanna

The Prophets Graphically Presented

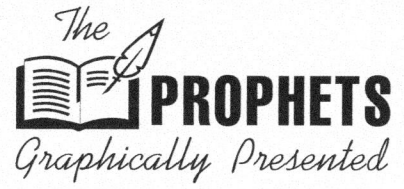

AMOS

Key Words:
*This is what the Lord says,
You have not,
Sins, Woe,
Chosen,
Seek*

Key Verse: 4:12, *Therefore ...because I will do this to you, prepare to meet your God, O Israel.*

Prologue	Announcing Judgment Against			Restoration Promised
	Eight Oracles	Three Sermons	Five Visions	
1 — 2	3	— 6 / 7	— 9:10	9:11-15
Gentiles, Judah, Israel	Israel		Israel, Gentiles, Judah	
"for three sins, even for four, I will not turn back my wrath"	"hear this word..."		"this is what the Sovereign LORD showed me"	
Judgment against: 1. Syria 2. Philistia 3. Phoenicia 4. Edom 5. Ammon 6. Moab 7. Judah 8. Israel [Certainty → Cause → Character]	Sermons re: Israel's: Doom 3 Depravity 4 Dirge 5-6 Three laments for: Righteousness lost Hypocrisy Complacency		Visions of Judgment 1. Locusts – averted 2. Fire – averted 3. Plumbline – determined (interlude – opposition) 4. Ripe fruit – imminent 5. God – altar – executed	Exiles will return and rebuild. Israel will be restored, at rest.

Amos 767–753 B.C. against Israel primarily

By Kenneth G. Hanna

OBADIAH

The Prophets Graphically Presented

Key Words:

In that day,

Do not ...,

Violence,

Disaster,

Possess

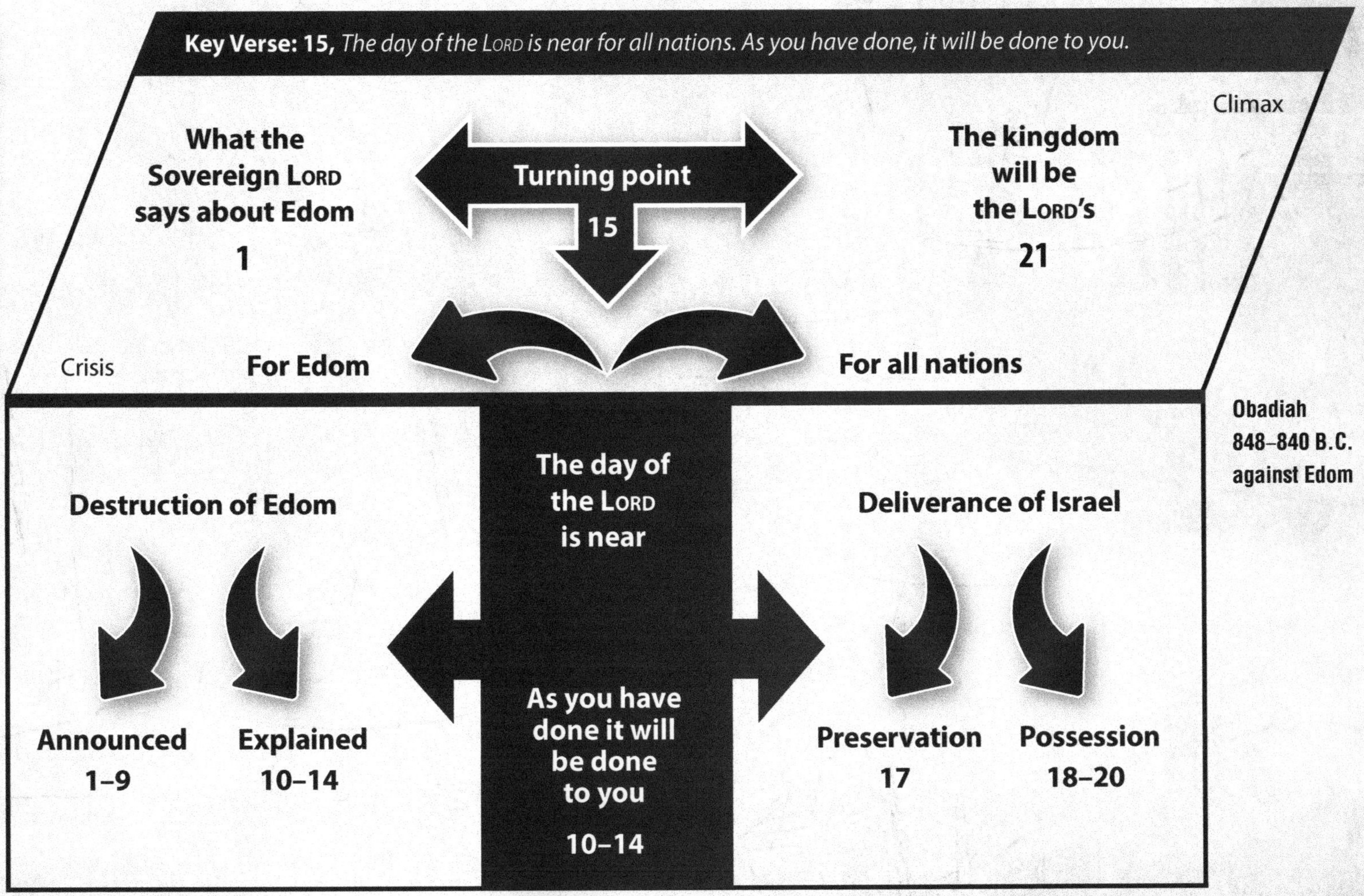

Key Verse: 15, *The day of the LORD is near for all nations. As you have done, it will be done to you.*

Crisis → Climax

What the Sovereign LORD says about Edom — 1

Turning point — 15

The kingdom will be the LORD's — 21

For Edom / For all nations

Destruction of Edom
- Announced 1–9
- Explained 10–14

The day of the LORD is near

As you have done it will be done to you — 10–14

Deliverance of Israel
- Preservation 17
- Possession 18–20

Obadiah 848–840 B.C. against Edom

By Kenneth G. Hanna

JONAH

Key Words:

Compassion,
Nineveh,
Provided,
Relent,
Turned,
Angry,
Right

Key Verse: 4:2, *You are a gracious and compassionate God, a God who relents from sending calamity.*

Jonah's First Comission		Jonah's Second Comission	
1 Go to Nineveh	2	3 Go to Nineveh	4
Yahweh's Compassion toward: Pagan Sailors, Jonah		Yahweh's Compassion toward: Nineveh, Jonah	
Jonah Running Away from God	Jonah Turning Back to God	Jonah Walking With God	Jonah Sulking Before God
Miracles — Great storm, Great calm, Great fish	Jonah preserved — Jonah on dry land	Nineveh's repentance — Nineveh's deliverance	Vine — Worm

Should I not be concerned about that great city?

Do you have a right to be angry?

Jonah
About 760 B.C.
israel

By Kenneth G. Hanna

THE PROPHETS Graphically Presented: MICAH

Key Words:
- Listen/hear,
- Remnant,
- People(s),
- Nation(s),
- Jacob,
- Zion,
- Walk

Key Verse: 7:18, *Who is a God like you, who pardons sin and forgives the transgression of the remnant?*

- **1st Message – Punishment**
- **2nd Message – Protest & Promise**
- **3rd Message – Pardon**

Listen!

Micah 735–700 B.C. against Judah

1 – 2	3 – 5	6 – 7
O peoples, all you	Leaders of Jacob, rulers of Israel	mountains, city!
Sin ➡ Judgment	Rebuke ➡ Hope ➡ Renewal	Indictment ➡ Pardon
Sovereign LORD	God is: Righteous Judge / True Shepherd	Redeemer / Pardoner
Idolatry of Judah will be judged 1:5 / Result of rebellion will be exile 1:16 / Future return is promised 2:12	Injustice in Zion will be judged 3:9 / Righteousness will be restored 4:2 / Divine, eternal, true shepherd will come out of Bethlehem 5:2, 4	God's requirement: Covenant obedience not offerings 6:8 / Hope rests in the pardoning God 7:18

By Kenneth G. Hanna

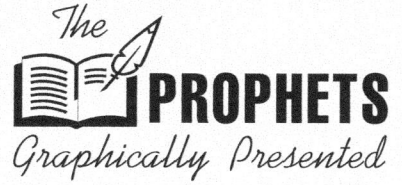

NAHUM

Key Words:
Anger, Wrath,
Vengeance,
No longer,
Guilty,
End

Key Verses: 1:7–8, *The Lord is good, a refuge in times of trouble ... He will make an end of Nineveh.*

Nineveh's Doom

Decreed — The Lord is an avenging God

Described

Deserved — Nineveh will be destroyed!

1	2	3
Psalm exalting the Judge	Chronicle describing judgment	Woe deserved by the accused
God, the Judge: Jealous, avenger, great in power, slow to anger, irresistible in wrath, good, refuge in times of trouble, cares for those who trust in him	**The Judgment:** Attacker advances, shields red, metal flashes, chariots rush, river gates are thrown open, Nineveh is pillaged, messengers are no longer heard	**Nineveh, the Judged:** City of blood, full of lies, plunder, never without victims, enslaver, mistress of sorceries, like locusts, who has not felt your cruelty?
Attributes of God, the Judge 1:2–7 → Verdict against Nineveh, the accused 1:8–14	Nineveh alerted 2:1 / God's intent to restore Judah 2:2 / Nineveh attacked and destroyed 2:3–12 / Justice served 2:13	First indictment 3:1–3 / Second indictment 3:4–7 / Third indictment 3:8–17 / Oppressed nations applaud outcome 3:18–19

Nahum 640–621 B.C. In Judah, but against Nineveh

By Kenneth G. Hanna

HABAKKUK

The Prophets Graphically Presented

Key Words:

*Violence,
Babylonians,
How long?,
Righteous will live by faith!,
Wait!*

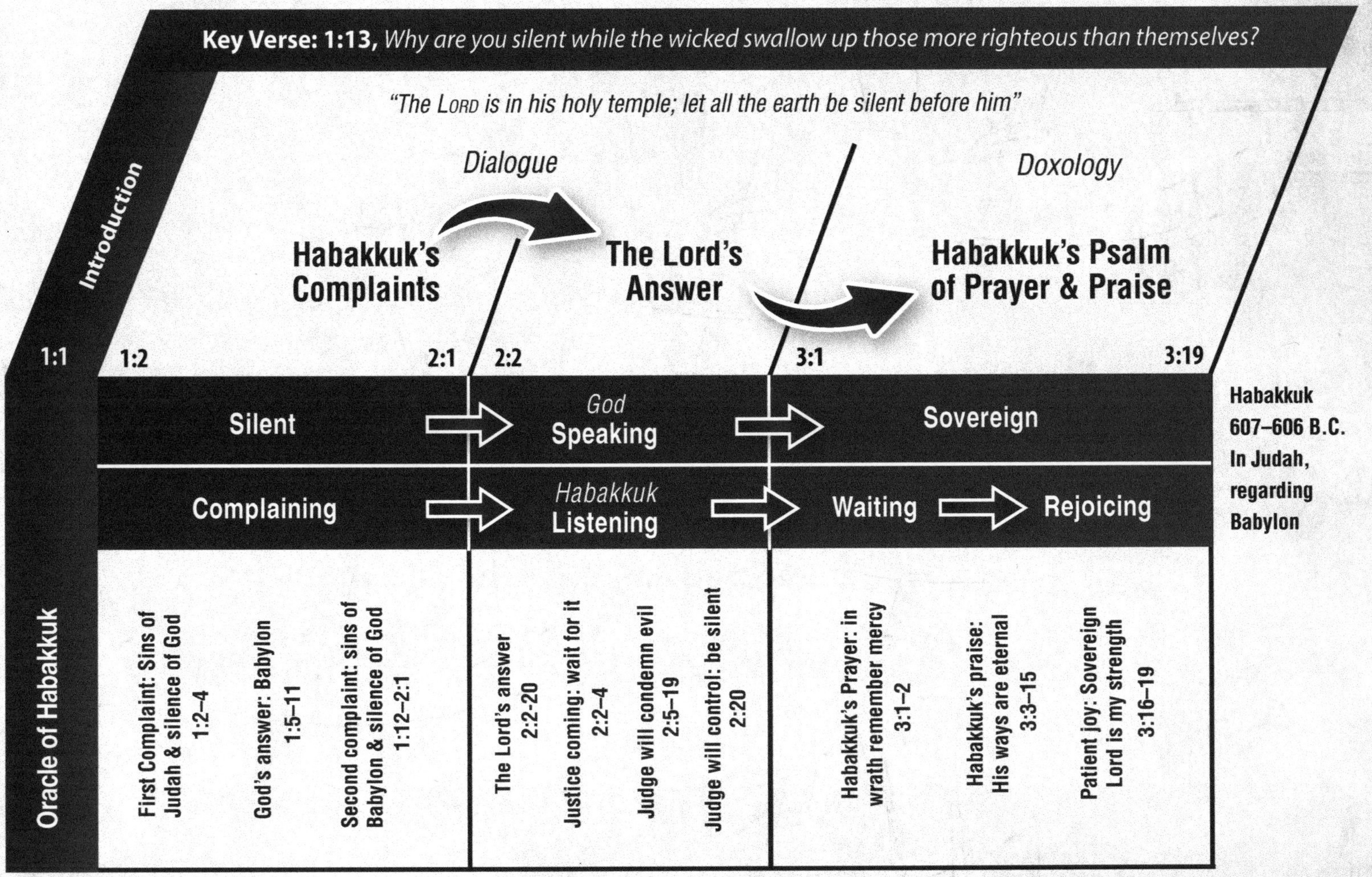

Key Verse: 1:13, *Why are you silent while the wicked swallow up those more righteous than themselves?*

"The LORD is in his holy temple; let all the earth be silent before him"

Dialogue — *Doxology*

Introduction | Habakkuk's Complaints → The Lord's Answer → Habakkuk's Psalm of Prayer & Praise

1:1 | 1:2 | 2:1 | 2:2 | 3:1 | 3:19

| Oracle of Habakkuk | Silent → | *God* Speaking → | Sovereign |
| | Complaining → | *Habakkuk* Listening → | Waiting → Rejoicing |

| First Complaint: Sins of Judah & silence of God 1:2–4 | God's answer: Babylon 1:5–11 | Second complaint: sins of Babylon & silence of God 1:12–2:1 | The Lord's answer 2:2 | Justice coming: wait for it 2:2–4 | Judge will condemn evil 2:5–19 | Judge will control: be silent 2:20 | Habakkuk's Prayer: in wrath remember mercy 3:1–2 | Habakkuk's praise: His ways are eternal 3:3–15 | Patient joy: Sovereign Lord is my strength 3:16–19 |

Habakkuk 607–606 B.C. In Judah, regarding Babylon

By Kenneth G. Hanna

ZEPHANIAH

Key Words: Day of the LORD, Anger, Wrath, Distress on Kingdoms, God will: gather, purify, Israel, Zion

Key Verse: 2:3, *Seek the LORD,... Seek righteousness... perhaps you will be sheltered on the day of the LORD's anger.*

God's wrath

The great day of the LORD is near!

God's joy

God's love

1:2 — 3:8 | 3:9 — 3:20

Judgment | Salvation

- 1:1 Introduction
- First cycle of oracles: Judgment
  - 1:2-3 Of man and all things
  - 1:4-2:3 Of Judah and Jerusalem
  - 2:4-15 Of nations around Judah
- Second cycle of oracles: Judgment
  - 3:1-7 Of the city of Jerusalem
  - 3:8 Of all nations and earth

God is mighty to save:
- 3:9 Invitation is to all
- 3:10 Remnant restored
- 3:11-13 Sin removed
- 3:14-17 King returned
- 3:18-20 Fortunes restored

Zephaniah 628–621 B.C. against Judah, Jerusalem, the nations

By Kenneth G. Hanna

HAGGAI

Key Words:
Give careful thought to your ways! Behold my house, Glory

Key Verses: 1:7–8, *Give careful thought to your ways... build the house, so that I may take pleasure in it and be honored.*

Four Messages

Give Careful Thought to Your Ways

Haggai
520 B.C.
Jerusalem

To Arouse	To Encourage	To Confirm	To Assure
1:1-15 35	2:1-9	2:10-19	2:20-23
August 29, *Consider your ways, build the temple.*	October 17, *Be strong and work, for I am with you.*	December 18, *Consider how things were before.*	December 18, *I will shake the heavens and the earth.*
Response *The people obeyed the voice of the Lord.*	**Promise** *I will fill this house with glory.*	**Promise** *From this day on I will bless you.*	**Promise** *I have chosen you*
Charge to start building the temple	Encouragement to finish building the temple	Temple finished, and dedicated in 516 B.C.	

Opens with a Problem 1:2 ⟷ Closes with a Promise 2:23

By Kenneth G. Hanna

ZECHARIAH

Key Words:

Lord Almighty,
Jerusalem,
On that day,
Shepherd,
King

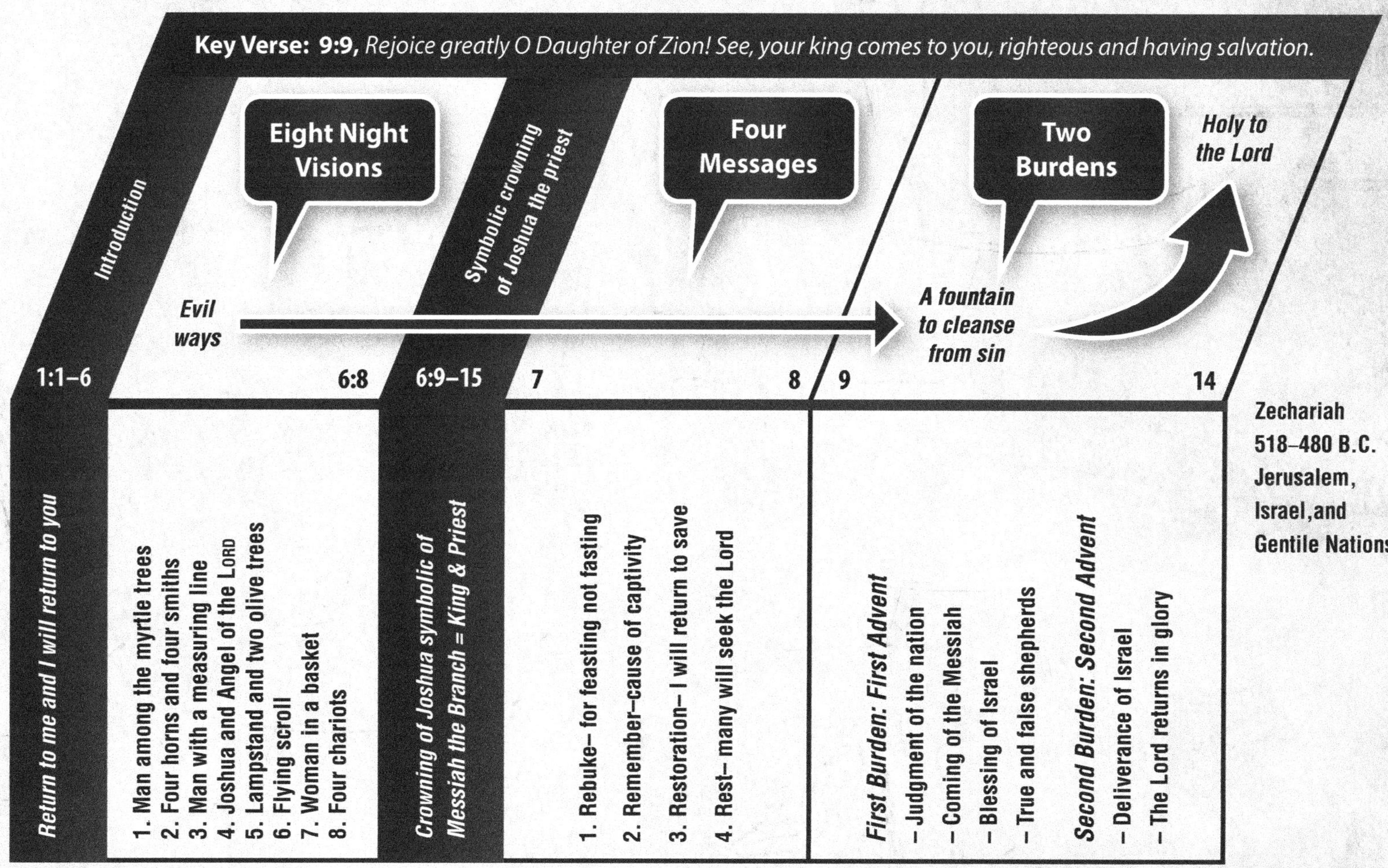

Key Verse: 9:9, *Rejoice greatly O Daughter of Zion! See, your king comes to you, righteous and having salvation.*

Eight Night Visions

Four Messages

Two Burdens

Holy to the Lord

Introduction

Symbolic crowning of Joshua the priest

Evil ways → A fountain to cleanse from sin

1:1–6 | 6:8 | 6:9–15 | 7 | 8 | 9 | 14

Zechariah 518–480 B.C.
Jerusalem, Israel, and Gentile Nations

Return to me and I will return to you

1. Man among the myrtle trees
2. Four horns and four smiths
3. Man with a measuring line
4. Joshua and Angel of the Lord
5. Lampstand and two olive trees
6. Flying scroll
7. Woman in a basket
8. Four chariots

Crowning of Joshua symbolic of Messiah the Branch = King & Priest

1. Rebuke— for feasting not fasting
2. Remember—cause of captivity
3. Restoration— I will return to save
4. Rest— many will seek the Lord

First Burden: First Advent
– Judgment of the nation
– Coming of the Messiah
– Blessing of Israel
– True and false shepherds

Second Burden: Second Advent
– Deliverance of Israel
– The Lord returns in glory

By Kenneth G. Hanna

MALACHI

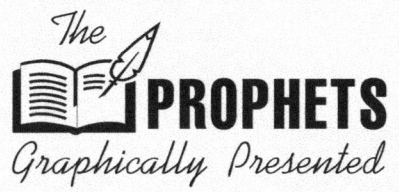

Key Words:
How have we?,
Messenger,
Covenant,
Return,
Revere

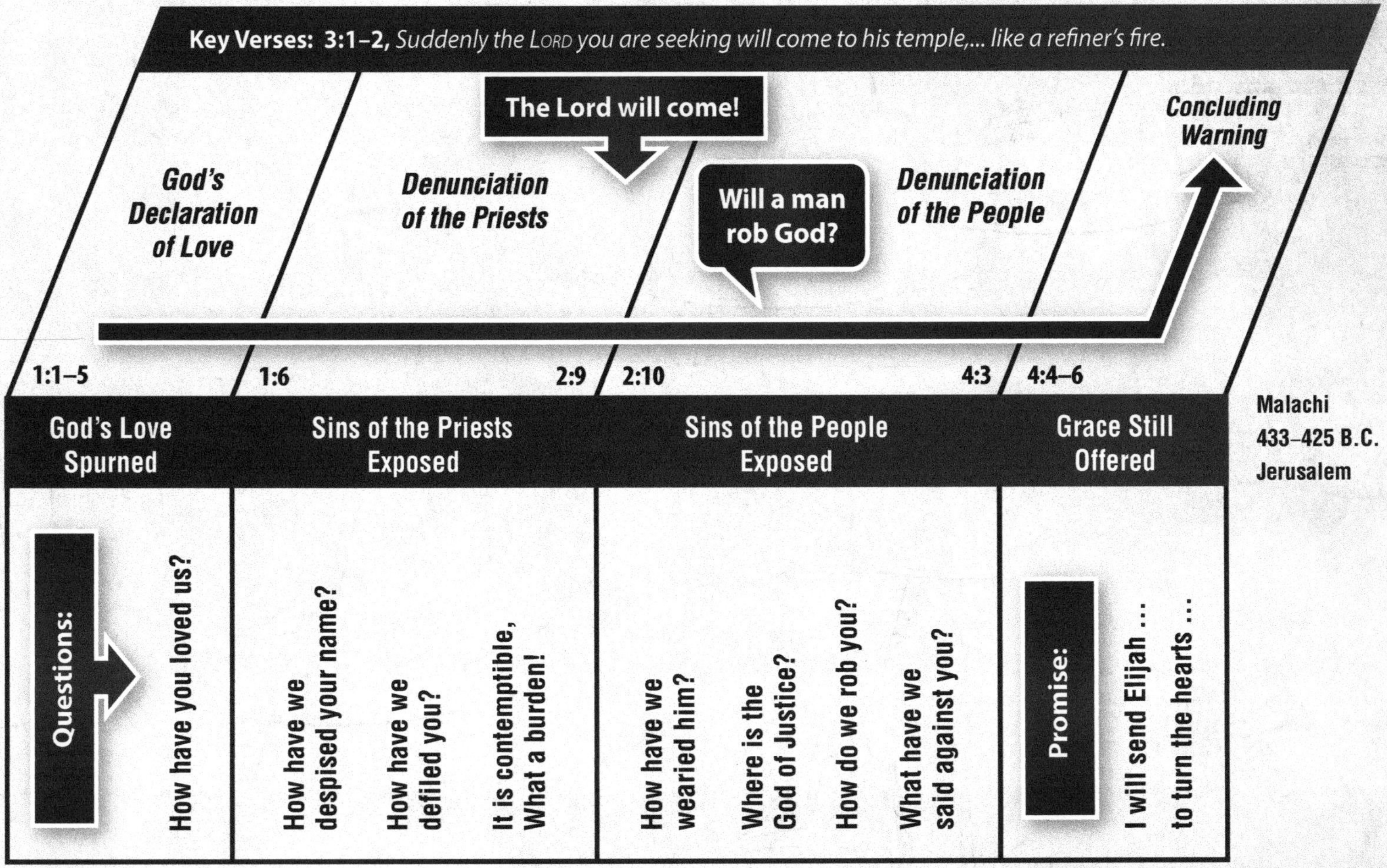

Key Verses: 3:1–2, Suddenly the LORD you are seeking will come to his temple,... like a refiner's fire.

1:1–5	1:6 – 2:9	2:10 – 4:3	4:4–6
God's Declaration of Love	Denunciation of the Priests	Denunciation of the People	Concluding Warning

The Lord will come! — Will a man rob God?

God's Love Spurned	Sins of the Priests Exposed	Sins of the People Exposed	Grace Still Offered
Questions: How have you loved us?	How have we despised your name? / How have we defiled you? / It is contemptible, What a burden!	How have we wearied him? / Where is the God of Justice? / How do we rob you? / What have we said against you?	**Promise:** I will send Elijah ... to turn the hearts ...

Malachi
433–425 B.C.
Jerusalem

By Kenneth G. Hanna

Dispensational Publishing House is striving to become the go-to source for Bible-based materials from the dispensational perspective.

Our goal is to provide high-quality doctrinal and worldview resources that make dispensational theology accessible to people at all levels of understanding.

Visit our blog regularly to read informative articles from both known and new writers.

And please let us know how we can better serve you.

Dispensational Publishing House, Inc.
PO Box 3181
Taos, NM 87571

Toll-Free 844-321-4202